A DREAM OF GOVERNORS

A
DREAM
OF
GOVERNORS

Poems by
LOUIS SIMPSON

Wesleyan University Press
MIDDLETOWN, CONNECTICUT

Some of these poems have appeared previously. I am indebted to the editors of the following publications in which poems have been published: *The American Scholar:* "The Flight to Cytherea," "An American in the Thieves' Market"; *The Arrivistes:* "Carentan O Carentan," "Rough Winds Do Shake," "Summer Storm," "The Custom of the World" (a revision of a poem in *The Arrivistes*); *The Columbia University Forum*: "Côte d'Azur"; *The Fifties:* "Carentan O Carentan"; *The Hudson Review:* "Orpheus in America," "The Runner," "The Bird"; *The London Magazine:* "Against the Age"; *New Poems by American Poets* (Ballantine Books): "The Silent Generation," "Tom Pringle"; *The New Yorker:* "The Green Shepherd," "A Dream of Governors," "The Legend of Success, the Salesman's Story," "Music in Venice," "Mediterranean," "The Lover's Ghost," "The Goodnight"; *Partisan Review:* "Hot Night on Water Street"; *The Paris Review:* "Orpheus in the Underworld," "The Boarder," "Old Soldier"; *Saturday Review:* "I Dreamed that in a City Dark as Paris," "Landscape with Barns" (originally titled "America"); *The Western Review:* "To the Western World," "The Traveler."

Library of Congress Catalog Card Number: 59–12480
Manufactured in the United States of America

First printing, September, 1959; fifth printing, 1982

To Dorothy

CONTENTS

1. THE GREEN SHEPHERD

The Green Shepherd   3

I Dreamed that in a City Dark as Paris   5

A Dream of Governors   6

Orpheus in the Underworld   8

The Flight to Cytherea   11

2. MY AMERICA

To the Western World   15

Hot Night on Water Street   16

Landscape with Barns   17

The Legend of Success,
      the Salesman's Story   18

The Boarder   20

Orpheus in America   21

3. THE OLD WORLD

An American in the Thieves' Market   25

Music in Venice   26

Côte d'Azur   28

Mediterranean   30

The Saints Are Feasting in Heaven   31

4. *THE RUNNER*

The Runner	**35**
Old Soldier	**67**
The Bird	**68**
The Silent Generation	**73**
Against the Age	**74**
Carentan O Carentan	**75**

5. *LOVE POEMS*

Rough Winds Do Shake	**79**
Summer Storm	**81**
The Traveler	**82**
The Custom of the World	**83**
The Lover's Ghost	**84**
The Goodnight	**85**
Tom Pringle	**87**

1. *THE GREEN SHEPHERD*

The Green Shepherd

Here sit a shepherd and a shepherdess,
He playing on his melancholy flute;
The sea wind ruffles up her simple dress
And shows the delicacy of her foot.

And there you see Constantinople's wall
With arrows and Greek fire, molten lead;
Down from a turret seven virgins fall,
Hands folded, each one praying on her head.

The shepherd yawns and puts his flute away.
It's time, she murmurs, we were going back.
He offers certain reasons she should stay—
But neither sees the dragon on their track.

A dragon like a car in a garage
Is in the wood, his long tail sticking out.
Here rides St. George, swinging his sword and targe,
And sticks the grinning dragon in the snout.

Puffing a smoke ring, like the cigarette
Over Times Square, Sir Dragon snorts his last.
St. George takes off his armor in a sweat.
The Middle Ages have been safely passed.

What is the sail that crosses the still bay,
Unnoticed by the shepherds? It could be
A caravel that's sailing to Cathay,
Westward from Palos on the unknown sea.

But the green shepherd travels in her eye
And whispers nothings in his lady's ear,
And sings a little song, that roses die,
Carpe diem, which she seems pleased to hear.

3

The vessel they ignored still sails away
So bravely on the water, Westward Ho!
And murdering, in a religious way,
Brings Jesus to the Gulf of Mexico.

Now Portugal is fading, and the state
Of Castile rising purple on Peru;
Now England, now America grows great—
With which these lovers have nothing to do.

What do they care if time, uncompassed, drift
To China, and the crew is a baboon?
But let him whisper always, and her lift
The oceans in her eyelids to the moon.

The dragon rises crackling in the air,
And who is god but Dagon? Wings careen,
Rejoicing, on the Russian hemisphere.
Meanwhile, the shepherd dotes upon her skin.

Old Aristotle, having seen this pass,
From where he studied in the giant's cave,
Went in and shut his book and locked the brass
And lay down with a shudder in his grave.

The groaning pole had gone more than a mile;
These shepherds did not feel it where they loved,
For time was sympathetic all the while
And on the magic mountain nothing moved.

I Dreamed that in a City Dark as Paris

I dreamed that in a city dark as Paris
I stood alone in a deserted square.
The night was trembling with a violet
Expectancy. At the far edge it moved
And rumbled; on that flickering horizon
The guns were pumping color in the sky.

There was the Front. But I was lonely here,
Left behind, abandoned by the army.
The empty city and the empty square
Was my inhabitation, my unrest.
The helmet with its vestige of a crest,
The rifle in my hands, long out of date,
The belt I wore, the trailing overcoat
And hobnail boots, were those of a *poilu*.
I was the man, as awkward as a bear.

Over the rooftops where cathedrals loomed
In speaking majesty, two aeroplanes
Forlorn as birds, appeared. Then growing large,
The German *Taube* and the *Nieuport Scout*,
They chased each other tumbling through the sky,
Till one streamed down on fire to the earth.

These wars have been so great, they are forgotten
Like the Egyptian dynasts. My confrere
In whose thick boots I stood, were you amazed
To wander through my brain four decades later
As I have wandered in a dream through yours?

The violence of waking life disrupts
The order of our death. Strange dreams occur,
For dreams are licensed as they never were.

A Dream of Governors

> The deepest dream is of mad governors.
> —MARK VAN DOREN

The Knight from the world's end
Cut off the dragon's head.
The monster's only friend,
The Witch, insulting, fled.
The Knight was crowned, and took
His Lady. Good and gay,
They lived in a picture-book
Forever and a day.

Or else: When he had sat
So long, the King was old
And ludicrous and fat.
At feasts when poets told
How he had shed the blood
Of dragons long ago
He thought, Have I done good
To hear that I did so?

The chorus in a play
Declaimed: "The soul does well
Keeping the middle way."
He thought, That city fell;
Man's life is founded on
Folly at the extreme;
When all is said and done
The City is a dream.

At night the King alone
Went to the dragon's cave.
In moonlight on a stone
The Witch sat by the grave.

6

He grasped her by the hand
And said, "Grant what I ask.
Bring evil on the land
That I may have a task!"

The Queen has heard his tread;
She shuts the picture-book.
The King stands by the bed.
In silence as they look
Into each other's eyes
They see a buried thing
That creeps, begins to rise,
And spreads the dragon's wing.

Orpheus in the Underworld

Night, dark night, night of my distress—
The moon is glittering with all the tears
Of the long silence and unhappiness
Of those who loved in vain for many years.

And so it glittered on the sleeping town
When Orpheus alone and sadly went
To death, to fetch Eurydice, and down
The fearful road pursued his dark descent.

Here were the walls, the gates where death had set
His warnings—in a city carved in stone
The citizens were busy; farmers whet
Their scythes in meadows never to be mown.

The kings and judges sat in their high places.
Then, at the sound of a loud trumpet blown,
They crowded, with pale terror on their faces,
From Death ascending to his dreadful throne.

Orpheus entered. As the eery light
Dwindled, he grasped his lute, and stumbling bent
His footsteps through the thick, enshrouding night.
Then suddenly, the lute by accident

Was struck—the sound exploded like a star
And shone and faded, and the Echoes woke
And danced, and ran before him. Down the far
Corridors it seemed the silence spoke.

He touched the strings again, began to play
In the same order. Fearfully he went
Toward the Echoes, and they still gave way.
And so he followed his own instrument.

At last to the deep hall of death he came.
And there the King sat, motionless and dread.
The night coiled from his nostrils like a flame;
The eyes lacked luster in the massive head.

And by his icy feet, pale in her shroud,
The beautiful Eurydice was laid.
Orpheus knelt beside her, and he bowed
His head, and touched the lute again, and played.

Night, dark night, night of my distress—
Once by the Mediterranean in May
I heard a nightingale, and the sadness of roses
In the murmuring wind, but this was sadder than they.

Night, dark night, night of my distress—
I too have waked her, seen the heavy shawl
Of night slip from her shoulders, and the darkness
Fly from her open eyes. And through the hall,

Through cities and the country of the dead
With the one I loved, hand in hand, have gone.
The dog of death was quiet as we fled,
And so we passed, as shadows over stone.

Under the hills in their enormous silence
And by the sea where it is always still,
I felt her hand in mine, the fearful sense
Of mortal love. And so we fled, until

I turned toward her. With a cry she vanished.
Goodbye, pale shadow of my happiness!
I to the light have been forever banished
That is the night, the night of my distress.

Then Orpheus pursued his lonely way
Upward into the world, and a strange glory
Shone from his face. The trees, when he would play,
Were moved, and roses wept to hear his story.

It's Orpheus in the wind. His music grieves
The moon. He tells the water of his loss.
And all the birds are silent, and the leaves
Of summer in that music sigh and toss.

The Flight to Cytherea

There are designs in curtains that can kill,
Insidious intentions in a chair;
In conversation, silence, sitting still,
The demon of decorum and despair.

Once, when I felt like that, I used to go
Abroad. I've made my marches drunk on night,
Hands in my pockets, pipe sparks flying so,
A liner to the tropics of the light.

Night is the people's theater, sad and droll.
There are the lovers, leaning on each other;
The businessmen, out for a little stroll
With their success; the bum who calls you brother.

And then, I've flown. I've risen like a sail,
A plane—the roads beneath shone bright and bare—
A black umbrella cracking in the gale
Over an ocean blank as a nightmare.

And came to Paris. I'm not talking of
Your chestnut blossoms, but the soldier's town,
The Butte, the calvados, odors of love,
Where for a little while I settled down.

In Africa I was. Beneath my wings
The lions roared. I floated on tobacco;
I made the eyeballs of the savage kings
Roll up. I spent a fortune at Monaco.

Then off again, to heights where the air fails,
The Alps are only shadows to the West,
That patch is India, the den of whales
A puddle—Ecstasies on Everest!

And glided out beyond the atmosphere
Toward the moon. It trembled like a bell.
"Step right up, gentlemen!" Then sudden fear
Opened. I felt the precipice. I fell.

Down down like an umbrella I unfurled
My bones. I must have fallen for a week;
Then slowly and more slowly as the world
Unwrinkled, valley, plain and mountain peak.

And fell into the country of your eyes,
Since when I have lived comfortably here;
My thoughts are only clouds in summer skies,
And everything is perfect, calm and clear.

2. MY AMERICA

To the Western World

A siren sang, and Europe turned away
From the high castle and the shepherd's crook.
Three caravels went sailing to Cathay
On the strange ocean, and the captains shook
Their banners out across the Mexique Bay.

And in our early days we did the same.
Remembering our fathers in their wreck
We crossed the sea from Palos where they came
And saw, enormous to the little deck,
A shore in silence waiting for a name.

The treasures of Cathay were never found.
In this America, this wilderness
Where the axe echoes with a lonely sound,
The generations labor to possess
And grave by grave we civilize the ground.

Hot Night on Water Street

A hot midsummer night on Water Street—
The boys in jeans were combing their blond hair,
Watching the girls go by on tired feet;
And an old woman with a witch's stare
Cried "Praise the Lord!" She vanished on a bus
With hissing air brakes, like an incubus.

Three hardware stores, a barbershop, a bar,
A movie playing Westerns—where I went
To see a dream of horses called *The Star*. . . .
Some day, when this uncertain continent
Is marble, and men ask what was the good
We lived by, dust may whisper "Hollywood."

Then back along the river bank on foot
By moonlight. . . . On the West Virginia side
An owlish train began to huff and hoot;
It seemed to know of something that had died.
I didn't linger—sometimes when I travel
I think I'm being followed by the Devil.

At the newsstand in the lobby, a cigar
Was talkative: "Since I've been in this town
I've seen one likely woman, and a car
As she was crossing Main Street, knocked her down."
I was a stranger here myself, I said,
And bought the *New York Times,* and went to bed.

Landscape with Barns

The barns like scarlet lungs are breathing in
Pneumonia. The North wind smells of iron.
It's winter on the farm. The Hupmobile
That broke its back is dying at the fence.
At night in a thin house we watch TV
While moonlight falls in silence, drop by drop.

The country that Columbus thought he found
Is called America. It looks unreal,
Unreal in winter and unreal in summer.
When movies spread their giants on the air
The boys drive to the next town, drunk on nothing.
Youth has the secret. Only death looks real.

We never die. When we are old we vanish
Into the basement where we have our hobbies.
Enough, when something breaks, that widows mourn
"He would have fixed it. He knew what to do."
And life is always borrowing and lending
Like a good neighbor. How can we refuse?

The Legend of Success, the Salesman's Story

The legend of success, the salesman's story,
Was finished in the shadows of the day.
Then Peter spoke: "There also is a glory
In failure, in a virtue cast away.
The optimistic fellow in your story
Comes home; my heroes march the other way.

"My first is Courage, and God only knows
His name. I saw his picture once, a death
By Brady—in the Devil's Den—old clothes
And an enormous gun; his only wreath
Dry nettles. But, I tell you, his repose
Was large. He made the silence hold its breath.

"My next is Knowledge. Tie an empty can
To a dog's tail, and hear the welkin howl.
One afternoon in Eden, there began
The terror and the journey of his soul—
Adam or Ishmael, the running man . . ."
He fiddled with his pipe and filled the bowl.

"My third is Magic. He had got the hang
Of words. That age has vanished out of speech,
But in Fitzgerald's fable, as they sang,
The sirens still are fading on the beach.
He glittered and collapsed, a paper bang
At the last party given by the rich."

He lit his pipe. "The other side of glory
Is dark—and still it beckons, like Cathay.
The satisfaction of a happy story
Leaves me nowhere to go."

"Well, anyway,"
The salesman said, "I like a happy story.
But each one to his taste, I always say."

The Boarder

The time is after dinner. Cigarettes
       Glow on the lawn;
Glasses begin to tinkle; TV sets
       Have been turned on.

The moon is brimming like a glass of beer
       Above the town,
And love keeps her appointments—"Harry's here!"
       "I'll be right down."

But the pale stranger in the furnished room
       Lies on his back
Looking at paper roses, how they bloom,
       And ceilings crack.

Orpheus in America

Here are your meadows, Love, as wide as heaven,
Green spirits, leaves
And winds, your ministers!

Item: a ship, that on the outer shoals
Lies broken. Item: thirty-seven souls,
Or rather, thirty-seven kinds of fever.
Item: three Indians, chained leg to leg.
Item: my lute.

This is the New England—rocks and brush
Where none may live but only tigers, parrots,
And mute imagining—
America, a desert with a name.

America begins antiquity.
Confronted with pure space, my Arcady
Has turned to stone.
Rome becomes Rome; Greece, Greece; the cottages
Collapse in ruin.

It darkens like a lapse of memory.
Here are no palaces, but lifted stone,
The pyramids of Egypt, steles
Of Ur. Columns that death has set
At the entrance to his kingdom.

II

This gazing freedom is the basilisk.
O for a mirror!
The melancholy of the possible
Unmeasures me.

Let music then begin. And let the air
Be passing sweet,
Music that scarcely wakes
The serpent in her trance
And leads the lion out into the dance.
And let the trees be moved,
And may the forest dance.

Then shall intelligence and grace
Join hands and sing: Goodbye to Arcady!
Another world is here, a greener Thrace!
Here are your meadows, Love, as wide as heaven,
Green spirits, leaves
And winds, your ministers,
In this America, this other, happy place.

3. THE OLD WORLD

I want to travel in Europe, Alyosha, I shall set off from here. And yet I know that I am only going to a grave-yard, but it's a most precious grave-yard, that's what it is! Precious are the dead that lie there, every stone over them speaks of such burning life in the past, of such passionate faith in their work, their truth, their struggle and their science, that I know I shall fall on the ground and kiss those stones and weep over them; though I'm convinced in my heart that it's long been nothing but a grave-yard.

The Brothers Karamazov

An American in the Thieves' Market

In Italy the dead have all the passion.
They still reverberate among the broken
Columns and stones. And in comparison
    The living seem
Content, in the light-garlanded piazza,
To stare at beauty, strolling with no aim
Between the silly fountains and the dim
    Forgetful stream.

If I were an Italian, I'd pinch
Life on the thigh—"*Buon giorno!*"—with a smile.
This is my business day: the offered bribe,
    Which I decline,
Then pocket—putting something in the glove
Of the police. At noon, enough of this.
And my old age is gazing, with my mistress,
    Cigars and wine.

But I am American, and bargain
In the Thieves' Market, where the junk of culture
Lies in the dust—clay shards, perhaps Etruscan,
    And wedding rings. . .
My father's ghost is ticking in a watch,
My mother's, weeping in the antique bed,
And, in a pile of swords, my cousins shed
    The tears of things.

Music in Venice

Dismiss the instruments that for your pleasure
Have played allegro all through Italy.
Pay the musicians. Even let the poet
    Have part his pay.
For here is Venice—floating, and suspended
From purple clouds. Dismiss the music school!
Here anyone at all can play the fool
    In his own way.

Then thread the labyrinth of narrow streets,
Bridges, canals, windows of lace and glass,
High lattices that spill the scent of almonds.
    The Minotaur
That lurks in this maze is kind. An Aschenbach
Round every corner is pursuing Eros.
"Love!" cry the naked offspring of the heroes
    On the wet stone floor.

It's night in the Piazza. Lighted space
Burns like your brandy. Violins and brass
Play waltzes, fox-trots. On a cloud, St. Mark's
    Winged lion perches;
High palaces go sailing to the moon,
Which, as advertised, is perfectly clear.
The lovers rise, moon-struck, and whisper their
    Arrivedercis.

A prince of Venice, tangled in the eyes
Of a young courtesan, once staged a masque:
"The Banishment of Love." A boy like Eros
    Was rowed in chains,
Weeping, down the canal. The merchant's Venice
Splintered the Turk and swept him from her shores.

But Eros came, Eros with many oars,
    And Eros reigns.

Venice, the city built on speculation,
Still stands on it. Love sails from India
And Sweden—every hanging cloud pours out
    A treasure-chest.
It's love on the Rialto, news of love,
That gives Antonio his golden life,
Even to Envy, sharpening a knife,
    His interest.

Christian says, "You know, it's Paradise,"
Mending his net.
"The English," he says, "for example . . .
They come and lie in the sun until they are
As red as that roof.
And then it's finished. They never recover."

The howling native children,
Roland, Giorgio, Josette, plunge in the sea,
Scramble on a raft, inspect
The official from Lyons with his glass rod
And nylon gear.
                    "I know," Roland informs him,
"Where you could have bought all that much cheaper.
That's not much of a rod."
                              "And you,"
Replies the head of the bureau
To his tormentor, "What kind of a rod
Do *you* have?"
                    Roland shrugs.
"Me?" he says. "I don't have all that money."

And here comes an excursion *en famille*.
First, they erect a yellow canvas tent
Which swallows them. Then mama-pig comes out
On her white trotters; whining daughter-pig;
Boy-pig and Baby. Look, the blossoming
Of beach-umbrellas, uncollapsing of chairs!
And last emerges the head of the family,
His face encased in glass, his feet
Froglike in flippers.
Out of his head a kind of **man-from-Mars**

Tube curls; his right hand grasps a trident
For finding the sea-urchin. *Me voici!*

Here and there on the beach the solitary
Brood in the sun—Dutchman and Swede;
An actress in dark glasses
Reading a book; heroes and heroines
Of melodramas that are to be played:
The shot in the hotel; the speech
From a platform; the performance
Of Bach that brings the audience to their feet
Roaring in Dusseldorf.

Humankind, says the poet, cannot bear
Too much reality.
                    Nor pleasure.
And nothing is more melancholy
Than to watch people enjoying themselves
As much as they can.
                    The trick is to be busy
Mending your net, like Christan,
Or active as the father is out there
With all his tackle.

                    Look! he's caught

An octopus.

                    The children come running,
And even the Swede
Stands up to look; the actress
Smiles; and the official from Lyons
Forgets himself in the general excitement.

Mediterranean

The evening, like a millionaire,
Is glittering, expansive, calm;
The moon will not fail to appear
Between a palm tree and a palm;
The planets and the speeding stars
Arrive like little foreign cars.

Those lights across the bay are Cannes.
They're having a film-festival—
Movies from Italy, Japan.
Believe me, I have seen them all.
And from the villas on the shore
I hear the television roar.

America, a female sage
Remarked, is old. We were the first
To enter on the modern age.
So history has been reversed,
And Europeans will discover
Our follies when we give them over.

And since this is the case in France,
I have obtained a rubber boat.
As these advantages advance
I'll grow increasingly remote.
The water laps around the bow.
Goodbye. For I am leaving now.

The Saints Are Feasting in Heaven

You saints, whose virtue was to bleed,
To lose an arm, an eye, a head,
Here is the harvest of that seed;
The feast of Paradise is spread.

Martyr, pick up your broken skull
And boldly take your place to dine.
Eat, eat, and yet be never full!
These delicacies are divine.

To give you music with your meat
The damned are burned and flayed with whips.
These are the proud who used to eat
The world, and wash their fingertips.

As with the Church, your naked spouse,
You lie through the unending night,
The sinners' knocks, locked from the house,
Renew the edge of your delight.

You saints, whose virtue was to bleed,
To be thrust back, rejected, cursed
By Pride and Luxury and Greed,
The last of all, shall be the first.

4. THE RUNNER

The Runner

This is the story of a soldier of the 101st. Airborne Division of the Army of the United States.

The Runner is fiction; the episodes and characters are imaginary. But the fiction is based on the following history.

On September 17, 1944, parachute and glider infantry of the First British Airborne Division, the American 82nd. and 101st. Airborne Divisions, and a Polish brigade, descended in eastern Holland, at Eindhoven, Grave, Nijmegen and Arnhem. Their object was to make a bridgehead across the Lower Rhine at Arnhem. The British Second Army would join them and advance from Arnhem into the plains of northern Germany.

At Arnhem the British airborne troops were attacked by enemy units in overwhelming strength, and forced back across the river. The more fortunate Americans defended a corridor from Eindhoven to Nijmegen. The fighting, bitter at first, settled into a stalemate, and, with the coming of the rainy season, petered out entirely.

In mid-November the 82nd. and 101st. were drawn back to Rheims, to re-equip and get the drizzle out of their bones.

On December 17, they were alerted for combat. A German attack was developing in Belgium. The divisions were hurried by truck into the Ardennes, and on the night of December 19, the 101st. were digging in around Bastogne.

I am most grateful to Mr. Donald Hall, who encouraged me to begin and to complete this story.

I

"And the condemned man ate a hearty meal,"
The runner said. He took his mess-kit over
To the garbage can. He scraped his mess-kit out,
Then dipped it in the can of soapy water,
And swished it in the can of clean, hot water,
And came back to his place.

              The company
Was spread along one edge of the airfield,
Finishing lunch. Those with the appetite
Were going through the chow-line once again.
They looked all pockets, pockets and baggy pants.
They held their mess-kits out to the sweating cooks,
Who filled them up; then bore their precious load
Apart.

        The runner felt in his breast-pocket
For cigarettes. He lit one and inhaled.
Leaning back on his pack, his feet sprawled out,
He stared at the ranks of gliders and tow-planes
And said, "I wonder if . . ."

              "Agh!" said a voice,
"Why don't you dry up, Dodd!"

             He looked around
And met the eyes of Kass, the radio-man,
Glaring beneath the rim of his steel-helmet.

"What?" said the runner.

          "Who needs your remarks?
First, the condemned men eat a hearty meal,
And then you wonder . . ."

"When we're coming back."

"What's it to you?"

                 The runner didn't answer.
Sometimes it seemed that anything he said
Rubbed someone the wrong way. He'd only meant
He hoped the outfit would come back to England.
He liked the village where they had been quartered,
And London, where he'd gone on two-day passes.
He liked the pubs, the mugs of mild-and-bitter,
And country lanes. Some day, when they came back,
He'd go off on his own. Rent a bicycle.
He'd see some of the country by himself.
And if he got to London . . .

                  With a roar
An engine started. Other engines followed.
A gale from the propellers swept around him.

"Fall in!" said the First Sergeant.

                   Dodd got up
And hoisted on his pack.

            "Get a move on!"

That's how it was: you always had to wait,
And then you had to hurry. He closed his belt,
And slung his rifle over his right shoulder.
The section formed.

           "Where's Wheeler?" said the sergeant.
And here came Wheeler at a run. "You, Wheeler . . ."

37

The sergeant followed him with imprecations
As Wheeler ducked in place at Dodd's right hand.
Out of the side of his mouth: "Look what I got,"
Said Wheeler, and he showed in his clenched fist
A bundle of the new invasion money.
"Over in F Company," he whispered.
"The dice was really hot."

                   "Ten-*hut!* For-*ard
Arch!*" said the sergeant, and they started off
Across the concrete runway. It seemed long.
Dodd's mouth was dry; his legs were weak. At last
They came up to the glider, their box-kite—
High wings and rudder, little wheels that hardly
Lifted it off the ground—a canvas coffin.
Ungainly as a duck, it wouldn't fly
Unless it had to.

                Through the open door
Under the wing, they climbed up one by one,
Toppling with their burdens. Found their seats.
And sat in two rows, looking at each other.
Dodd fastened his safety belt and clasped his gun
Between his knees. The Captain entered last.
They waited. The glider trembled in the blast
Of wind from the tow-plane. The pilots entered,
Leaping up lightly, and made their way forward
To the controls.

              The runner could see nothing
Beyond the glider's high, transparent nose;
But now, he thought, the tow-plane would be turning

Into the wind. Two men would run the cable
Back from the plane and hook it to the glider.
Then, with a louder blast of the propellers,
The plane would start to roll.

                    The glider jerked
Forward, and rolled, creaking, and gathered speed.
The bumping stopped, and with a sudden lightness
They were air-borne. Constricted where he sat,
Dodd prayed to nothing in particular:
Let the rope hold; no current whirl us down
Smashing on concrete.

              They were well away.
He stared at the slender pilots in their pinks
And sporty caps and glasses; at their hands
On the half-wheel. His life was in those hands.
He thought of shell-bursts, the green canvas torn,
Men writhing in their belts, the pilots' hands
Fallen from the controls, a sickening drop.
And then he thought of fields with pointed stakes
That would shear through the sides. Of plunging out
Into machinegun fire.

II

            "We're almost there,"
The next man said.

             The pilots were peering down.
One nodded, and the other raised his hand
And grasped the lever that released the cable,
And pulled it down.

The glider soared, then fell
Slanting away. The wing rose up again.
They glided down on silence and the wind.

The fields were rushing at them, tilted steep.
Dodd braced himself. The glider leveled, lightly
Bumped on the ground, and rolled to a dead stop.

The door was open. They were climbing through.
And now were standing in an open field
Flat as a pancake. Gliders strewed the scene.
Others were skimming down; and still the sky
Was filled with gliders.

From their lifted bows
The gliders were disgorging jeeps and cannon.
Riflemen formed their files and marched away.
Dodd's section took its place in the company.
The Captain raised his arm; he swept it down,
And they were marching.

On the bright horizon
A windmill stood. The land was crossed with dykes.
It looked like a Dutch painting. To their left
A wood began. They marched in that direction.

The day was hot, and Dodd began to sweat.
Then to his ears came the familiar sound
Of guns, the battle-roll, continuous.
Then all his other days were like a dream.
This was reality: the heat, the load
Strapping his shoulders, and the sound of guns.

The war, after Normandy, had seemed remote.
He had been there; his courage had been proved
To his own satisfaction. He had listened
To talk about the fighting, and he'd talked
And lost the sense of truth. He had forgotten
The smell of apples and the fear of death.
Now he remembered. And it seemed unjust
That he should be required to survive
Again. The sound increased. The battleground
Looked ominous. Visions of a huge mistake
Struck at his heart.

III

The company was entering the woods.

"Dodd," said the sergeant, "take this message up
To Lieutenant Farr."

       He stepped out of the file
And hastened to the front. The lead platoon
Was walking slowly, with the scouts ahead.
He gave the message.

       "Right," said the lieutenant.
The runner started back. As he went by
Faces stared into his inquiringly.
He seemed possessed of an important secret.

Shots went off behind him. He crouched and swung
Out of the path, and lay in the scrub, face down.
The firing stopped. A voice was calling "Medic!"

Fisher, a sergeant of the third platoon,
Came up the path, bent low. He shook Dodd's shoulder:
"Who's doing all the shooting?"

                      "I don't know,"
Dodd said. The sergeant, with a grim expression,
Stared at him, and went on.

                         The runner waited.
Why didn't they get it over with!

                      "Move out!"

He got to his feet. The path filled up with men.
He made his way back, past the sweating faces
Now streaked with dust. He fell in with his section,
Turned round, and traveled up the path again
He'd just traversed.

                The files ahead were parting.
The men looked down, as into a precipice.
There was a body lying in the way.
It was Santelli, of the first platoon.
Dodd had just seen him going out in front;
He walked like a dancer, with a short, neat step,
Rifle held crosswise.

                He lay huddled up
On his left side; his helmet had rolled off;
His head was seeping blood out in the dirt.

The files ahead were lagging; then they hurried.
"Keep your intervals!" the Captain shouted.
They hated him together.

At the break
They sprawled out of the path, in the underbrush.
Santelli's death had made them strangely silent.
Their helmets bowed their heads down on their chests.
Under the distant thudding of the guns,
The weight of all their burdens and the sky,
They couldn't speak, or stir themselves, or lift
A cigarette.

       Dodd thought about Santelli.
One of the afternoons it seemed forever
All they would do was practice for the war
With marches, tactics and map exercises,
He lay beneath the wall of an English garden,
Sucking a stalk of grass, and watched the clouds,
And far above the clouds, a fleet of bombers
Trailing long plumes of white across the blue.
Close by, Santelli sat, paring his nails
With a pocketknife.

            "Hey, runner-boy," he said
In the familiar and sneering tone
That Dodd despised. "What're we doin, hey?
You've been to college, right?" His little eyes
Were sharp with mockery—a little man
Of pocketknives and combs. "You ought to know.
What's it all about?"

IV

A plane flew glittering out of the sun—
A *Thunderbolt*. It swooped and disappeared
Behind a screen of trees. Then a staccato

43

Sound began. Machineguns. The plane rose
And flew away. They watched it till it vanished.

"On your feet," the sergeant said.

                          "My aching back!"
Someone said; but the gripe lacked conviction.
They stood and crumbled out their cigarettes,
And rolled the paper into little balls,
As though they'd like to keep the battlefield
Clean as a barracks.

                          As Dodd marched, the weight
Sawed at his shoulders: pack and ammunition,
Gas-mask and trench-tool, bayonet, grenades.
He plodded with clenched jaws, his eyes cast down
On the dusty path, the heels moving ahead.
He stayed, it seemed, in a fixed position;
It was the scene that moved.

                          The path reeled in
Another corpse. It came to him boot-first:
A German soldier on his back, spread-eagle,
A big, fresh-blooded, blond, jack-booted man
In dusty gray. Stepping around the fingers,
Around the bucket helmet, Dodd stared down.
A fly lit on the teeth. He looked away
And to the front, where other attitudes
Of death were waiting. He assumed them all,
One by one, in his imagination,
In order to prevent them.

Small-arms fire
Was crackling through the wood. Platoons spread out
In arrow-shaped formations.

"Dig in!"

He dug.
The shovel sank in sand; he hacked at roots.
Overhead, shells were whispering, and smoke
Came drifting back.

Two planes went whistling over.
Typhoons. They darted searching on the front.
They dived, and from their wings plunged rockets down
In smoking streaks. The ground shook with concussions.

"We're moving out!"

Dodd climbed out of the hole
That he had dug. The company moved in silence
Through the burning wood.

V

Beyond the wood there stretched an open road.
They filed out on it. In a field of hay
A plane perched on its nose, a *Messerschmidt,*
The black cross glaring.

Houses stood here and there.
In front of one, a mattress had been laid,
And on the mattress, a German officer.
He was puffed up with air like a balloon,
Belly and limbs swelling as if to split
His uniform. The grass was stuck with feathers.

Night was falling; the light had left the fields.
The road approached a village. At the entrance
A German half-track had been blown apart,
Its mustard-yellow metal torn and scorched;
Out of it spilled the crew, burned black as rubber.
The street, as they passed through, was strewn with dead,
A presentation of boot-soles and teeth,
Letters, cigars, the contents of their lives.

The cannonading was more loud, and flashes
Lit the darkening sky. A company
Of paratroopers passed them, coming back
With somber faces.

V I

Night. And the fields were still. The cannonade
Was flickering and grumbling through the sky.
Red flashes lined the clouds. No breath of wind
Was moving. In the holes that they had dug
The tired troops were sleeping on their arms.

"Dodd, get up!"

He struggled out of his bag.

The First Sergeant leaned over: "Take this message
Back to Battalion."

Dodd took the paper,
His helmet and his M-1, and set off,
Still half asleep.

Darkness without a moon
Surrounded him. He made his lonely way

Over a road that skirted trees and dykes.
The guns were rumbling; shells went fluttering over;
Machinegun tracers sparkled distantly.
A flare popped in the sky and glimmered down;
He waited in the shadow of a tree
Till it went out. And took the road again.

A deepening of black, a looming wall,
Was Battalion C. P. The guard called out:
"Halt! Who's there?"

                The runner spoke the password:
"Kansas!" and was admitted by the guard
Into the courtyard. There he gave his message
To a tech-sergeant; sat down on a bench,
And waited, looking at the pulsing sky.

"Runner!"

        He answered.

                 "Take this message back."

That was his job. Now all I need, he thought,
Is one of those Philip Morris uniforms
The bell-boys wear.

             The road was long and dark.
And it was weird to be alone in Holland
At midnight on this road. As he went on
He felt he had no weight. The landscape seemed
To have more things to think of than his journey.
These errands gave him little satisfaction.
Some men might think he led the life of Riley,

Safe and warm and dry, around Headquarters.
A man could be a runner all his life
And never be shot at. That's what they thought.
But how about the shelling? He'd been shelled
As much as anyone. And back in France,
At Carentan, he had been shot at—plenty!
It wasn't his fault he never had a chance
To fire back. Now, right here on this road,
He might be killed by accident. But still,
That wouldn't be the same as being brave.
He had no chance to be thought so, no part
In the society of riflemen.
So, as he went, he reasoned with himself.

VII

Next day the company went up on line
Near Veghel. They were digging round a church,
In the cemetery, and were just knee-deep
When hell broke loose.

                 The screaming and flat crack
Of eighty-eights.

          Air-bursts.

                 The metal slashed
The trees and ricocheted. Bit in the ground.

The runner on his belly lay contracting
Under the edge of metal. From a tree
A yard away, leaves flew.

                 A voice cried "Medic!"

His belly and his buttocks clenched each time
A shell came in. And they kept coming in.
He felt a sting between his shoulder blades.
I'm wounded! he thought, with a rush of joy.

"Dodd!" someone called.

                    He went on hands and knees
Toward the voice.

           "Over here," it urged him.

It was his sergeant, with a dozen cases
Of mortar shells.

           "Take them up to the mortars,"
The sergeant said. "They're out of ammunition."

He took two cases, one beneath each arm,
And ran off, dodging among the trees and graves.
He found the mortars and came running back
To get another load. The crack and hum
Of the artillery was all around him.
He felt the sting of the place where he'd been hit.
He knew that he was brave.

                On the last trip,
Kneeling above a mortar, as he lowered
The cases gently, one of the mortar crew
Said, "You're a good man, Dodd."

                  That night he lay
Smiling, without a care, beneath the sky.
He had done all that could be expected.

VIII

October, and the sky was turning gray.
The battle-line had settled. Every night
The bombers flew, going to Germany
At a great height. And back the other way
The V-1's came. The soldiers in their holes
Heard them droning and saw the rhythmic flames
Carrying woe to Antwerp and to England.

They dozed or watched. Then it began to rain,
And always rained. It seemed they were never dry.
Winter was in the air. Paths turned to mud.
By day and night the shells came shrieking in;
They got so they could tell a dying fall
And pay the rest no mind. They lived with mud.
They cooked and ate their rations in the can,
And tried to dry their socks between two rains.
Cold and sullen, under a raincoat roof,
They shivered in their holes.

                          One moonlit night
Dodd was returning on his way alone.
There was a wind; the haunted shadows stirred,
And rainpools glimmered in the moonlit fields.

There was a field the runner loathed to cross.
A place of horrors. Here, on the first day,
There'd been fierce charges, combats at close range,
And the dead were mixed as they had fallen.
Here crouched the German soldier with his *schmeisser*
Close to the parachutist in his rage—
Putrid things, never to be forgotten.
The field was swelling, shining with an aura
Of pale corruption.

                    To avoid it, Dodd
Went by another path he did not know,
Leading, it seemed, back to the company.
But in a while a fearful premonition
Stopped him. In a shadow, cold with dread,
He stood listening. The branches stirred,
And all at once there was a clash of arms,
The sound of footsteps. Stealthily he turned
To slip away.

                "Wer geht da?"

                        He ran.
He plunged into the darkness, blind with panic.
A storm of shots erupted at his back.
Brambles tore at his legs. He climbed a bank,
Clawing, and stumbled down the other side.
Then, as he ran, he shouted out the password:
"Ohio!" like a dog drenched with hot water.
His rifle fell. He left it where it was.
"Ohio!" He collided with a branch
And staggered. At his back the storm increased.
Red tracers streaked the air. Across a ditch
He leaped. And ran across the road beyond.
A hole was in his way; he cleared it with
A stride, and the dark figure starting up
Out of the hole. He kept on running, shouting
"Ohio!" A shape standing in the path
Snatched at him; he swerved out of its grasp.
There was a maze of holes. He stumbled, reeled,
And fell. His helmet flew off with a clang.

Feet were approaching. He lay still as death.

"It's Dodd," said a voice.

At last, he looked up
Into the faces of the third platoon.
Fisher. Others. They looked down in wonder.

I X

The regiment was bivouacked near Rheims
In tents on the bare plain. Wind-driven clouds
Streamed over, and the land in chilly streaks
Heaved like a sea. The wind hummed on the ropes
And whipped the tent flaps.

Dodd, stretched on his cot,
Could see and hear the third platoon at drill.
They turned to the flank and to the flank again;
They marched to the rear.

"Count cadence . . . cadence count!"

"Hup . . . two . . . three . . . four!" they answered on
the wind.
The sun flashed from the slanting rifle butts.

The corporal shouted: "When I say Ohio,
To the rear march, and double-time like hell!"
There was a burst of laughter, then: "Ohio!
Run!" the corporal said, *"Hup* . . . two . . . three . . .
four!
Halt! Now we'll try that movement once again.
When I give the word Ohio, turn around

52

And double-time as if your name is Dodd.
Make it look good. All right now—forward *'arch!*
Ohio!"

Dodd rolled over on his face.
He saw himself once more before the Captain:
"Screaming the password . . . throwing away your
            gun. . . .
Keep out of my sight, Dodd. You make me sick."

And then, the jokes, from reveille to sleep:
"That is Ohio, one of the midwest boys."
Replacements would be sent to see Ohio
To draw their running shoes. "I'm from Cleveland,"
One of them told him. "What part are you from?"

He turned upon his back. Right overhead
His jacket hung, with regimental ribbons,
The bronze star, and his shameful purple heart.
He stared at it. If he could only sleep
The time between, until the sergeant came
To put him on another hard detail!
That was his punishment: to dig latrines,
Pick cigarette butts up, scrub greasy pots—
Or to do nothing for a live-long day
But think and try to read, in a cold tent.

When the men came in, they would ignore him—

"You going in to town?"

                        "You said it, man!"

Polishing up their paratrooper boots
Until the toes reflected a lit match;

Blousing the trousers in their boot-tops; brushing
Their jackets; tucking ties between two buttons;
Cocking their caps—

"Let's go!"

He fell asleep,
And dreamed that he was climbing. On the crest
A dummy stood, with stiff, ballooning arms
And painted face, in Prussian uniform.
He reached the arms and swung them. It went "B-r-r-r-m!"
Like a machinegun. "B-r-r-r-m!" the sound came out
The dummy's painted lips and barrel belly.
Then he was walking over a green field.
It was a country he had never seen,
With haystacks, a warm wind, and distant barns.
Shadows were walking with him, and a voice
Spoke with the measure of a travelogue:
"*Vingtième Division* . . . fifty per cent . . ."
Another voice inquired: "Casualties?"
"No," said the first voice, "all of them are dead."
And it continued: "*Douzième Infanterie* . . .
Fifty per cent . . ." As the first voice was speaking,
Over the field, as on a movie screen,
Hands were imposed; they held a scarlet cloth
And folded it. "René de Gaumartin,"
The voice continued, "Cardinal of France."
Again the hands were folding a red robe.
"Marcel Gaumartin, Cardinal of France."
And as the voice and the pale hands continued
Their meditative play, Dodd came upon
A girl in black. She had fair hair and skin,

54

Plain features, almost ugly, but her eyes
Were large, they shot out tender rays of light.
The voice said, "Mademoiselle de Maintenon."
In his dream, Dodd laughed. *De Maintenon!* She said,
In a voice remote with sadness, "Yes," and smiled,
"I try not to think of them too much."

                                        He woke,
And his heart was light. It was a vision,
He thought. What does it mean? What eyes she had!
That field, with the wind blowing, and the clouds!
And yet, it was absurd. The words were nonsense.

He went out of his tent.

                        The third platoon
Were sitting down, taking a smoking break.
"Ohio!" someone shouted. "Where you running?"

He walked the other way, toward a rise
With trees, the only trees in all the plain,
Leaving the tents behind.

                        He climbed the slope
And sat beneath a tree. On the horizon
Rheims, with the cathedral, like a ship
Traveled the plain. Clouds were streaming over
The spire; their swift shadows ran like waves.
He lit a cigarette. Then, near at hand,
He saw the earth was trenched. A long depression,
No more than a foot deep, with rotten posts
And scraps of wire, wound across the slope.
He stood, and walked along it. The earth gave
Under his boots. He picked up a small scrap

Of wire, and it crumbled. He surmised
This was a trench dug in the first Great War.
Who knew? Perhaps an older war than that.
He faced the East, to Germany and Russia.
Shadows were standing with him. It was cold.
They watched, wrapped in old overcoats, forgotten.
They stamped their feet. The whole world was deserted
Except for them; there was nobody left.
On the imagined parapet, a cross
Howled in the wind; and there were photographs
Of girls and children; bunches of cut flowers.
Then, on the pitted, gaunt escarp, the night,
The melancholy night, swept with grandeur.
Far in the dark, star-shells were blossoming.
They stamped their feet. It was too cold. Too much
To expect of them. Their boots sank in the mud.
Their veins seemed ice; their jaws creaked with the cold.
They spoke; their words were carried on the wind,
Mingled, and lost.

    But now, an actual sound
Arrived distinctly. When he turned to look,
The camp was stirring; men ran to and fro.
He saw the third platoon halt in their drill,
Fall out, and run toward their tents. He moved;
He ground his cigarette out underfoot,
And hastened down the slope.

      "Where have you been?"
Said the First Sergeant.

      "I've been for a walk.
What's going on?"

           "Full field. Ready to move
In half an hour."

           Dodd's tent was in confusion.
The men were cramming rations in their packs,
Rolling their sleeping bags, cleaning their weapons.
He labored with stiff fingers.

                   Trucks drew up
Outside.

       "Get a move on!" a corporal shouted.

Dodd hitched on his pack.

              The company
Fell in and shuffled, straightening their ranks,
Eyes to the right.

         "Let's go!"

             Dodd took his place
In the line of olive-drab, the overcoats,
Helmets, packs, the gloved hands holding weapons.
The roll was called; he answered to his name.

They marched up to the trucks.

             "Mount up!"

                  He climbed
Into the truck, and was packed in. The gate
Clanged shut behind him.

                         57

X

Day turned to dusk; the truck went jolting on;
The wind was drumming on the canvas hood
And prying coldly down the runner's back.
Dusk turned to evening, and the trucks behind
Were hidden. He dozed off. Monotony
Had numbed his senses like an anesthetic.
When the gears shifted he would nearly wake.
Sometimes the truck would stop for no clear reason,
And faces, blinking in their woolen caps,
Lifted and muttered; someone tried to stretch,
And this set off a ripple of complaints.
Then the truck moved again.

                          Once they dismounted,
And Dodd saw that the road wound through a forest.
There was a hill on one side; on the other,
The trees descended into a ravine.
Against that bank, a group of people stood:
Women and children dressed in country black,
With kerchiefs round their heads, and an old man
Close by a cart. The cart was piled with things:
A mattress, pots and pans. They stood in silence
Watching the soldiers. Then the trucks re-loaded,
And the onlookers vanished.

                          They were driving
More slowly now. The men were all awake.
Another stop. Again the tail-gate opened,
And they dismounted.

                          This, then, was the place.
Colliding in the dark, they formed platoons,
And marched away.

A signpost read *Bastogne*.
They marched through a dark village with locked doors,
And were led off the road, into the woods.
The path was very dark, the march confused,
With frequent halts.

They halted in one place
Endlessly; they reclined, propped on their packs.
His helmet dragged Dodd's head back on his neck;
His feet got cold; under his woolen shirt
The sweat was trickling, then began to chill.

Then they were roused, pressed on without a pause,
Till, on a ridge commanding a black slope,
They halted. And the order came: "Dig in!"

Dodd unhitched his pack, laid it on the ground,
And leaned his rifle on it. From his belt
He took his trench-tool out, and opened it.
He stuck the shovel blade into the ground
And levered it. He'd barely circumscribed
A foxhole, when a cold chill touched his cheek—
Snow!

That's all we needed, the runner said
To the malignant sky.

From branch to branch
Snow glimmered down and speckled the dim ground.
Dodd dragged a fallen branch across his hole
And made a roof.

"Pack up," the sergeant said.
"We're moving out."

God help them, they were led
By officers and morons, who had orders
For wearing leather out and breaking spades,
To give employment to the men at home
Who, on this freezing night, were warm in bed
With soldiers' wives!

Having said so, they walked
On in the stumbling dark, till once again
They halted, in a place just like the first.

"Dig in!"

And it was useless, but they dug
With the energy of a supreme contempt
Marvelous holes—each clammy wedge of earth
An accusation flung in heaven's face.

Then, like a sound engendered by their mood,
An angry muttering rose on the night.
It faded, and again came to their ears—
The sound of guns.

At last, Dodd's hole was finished.
He lowered himself, rolled out his sleeping bag,
And pushed into it. Flickerings of light
Twitched overhead; the guns were coming closer.
Here, it was still. The snow came drifting down.

"Dodd, you're on guard."

He climbed out of his hole.

"There, by the trees."

He walked across the snow,
And as he went he looked around, astonished—
The sky was lit with spots of burning red
In a great circle.

As he stood on guard,
Surveying the black slope, the distant fires,
A man approached. Dodd challenged him. He spoke
The password, and came slogging through the trees.
A runner from Battalion. Brushing snow
Out of his neck, he asked for the C. P.
Dodd pointed: "Over there. Close to the barn.
What's happening now?"

"We're up a creek, that's what!
They're coming—panzers from the Russian front,
Under Von Runstedt. Panzers and SS.
I was just talking to a man who said
The line at St. Vith has been overrun
By tanks. It was a total massacre.
They're dropping paratroopers too," he said,
And turned away. He paused again to add:
"Everyone else is pulling out but us,"
And trudged away, leaving Dodd to his thoughts.

XI

The night was long. And day seemed less to rise
Than darkness to withdraw. Dodd, in his hole,
Could hear the fire of small arms, that seems
More threatening to the solitary man
Than does artillery.

                    One hole away
A helmet like a turtle shell was stirring.
A puffy face with whiskers turned around;
It was the mailman, Lopez. He arranged
Twigs on the snow. On these, his drinking mug.
He struck a match, applied it to the twigs,
And nursed the flame with cupped hands, bending over.

Under the hanging sky, congealed with clouds,
Fog trailed and clung to the earth; and the Ardennes,
The spectral firs, their branches cloaked with snow,
Stood stark against the foggy atmosphere.

Dodd stamped his feet. He stooped, and from his pack
Took a K-ration box. He tore it open,
Shook out the can of egg, the pack of biscuits,
The packet of coffee. He removed a glove
And with that hand put snow into his mug.
Poured coffee in, and mixed it with his spoon.
He scooped a hollow in the snow, and piled
Some twigs in it, and strips of the ration box.
And then put the mug on, and lit the pile.

Voices came floating up—loud gutturals;
A whine and clanking of machinery.
He picked his gun up.

                    At the foot of the slope
The trees were shaking, parting. There emerged
A cannon barrel with a muzzle-brake.
It slid out like a snake's head, slowly swinging.
It paused. A flash of light came from its head;
A thunder-clap exploded to Dodd's left;

Metal whanged on the slope, a spume of black
Hung in the air.

        Then, endlessly it seemed,
The barrel slid out. With a thrash of branches
A tank appeared. It lurched, seemed to consider,
And then came on, at an appalling rate.
The engine whined; the tracks jingled and squeaked.
And imperceptibly, out of the trees
Stood men, like apparitions of the snow.

And now it was a swarm of walking men
In field-gray and in white, with capes and hoods.

Dodd placed his elbows on the snow, took aim—
There was another thunder-clap. He ducked
And came upright again. To left and right
Rifles were firing. Hastily he pointed
The muzzle at a running, hooded shape,
And pressed the trigger. As in a nightmare
Nothing happened. A bullet cracked by his head.
The safety catch was on. He pressed it forward,
And aimed the gun again, and squeezed the trigger.
The butt kicked in his shoulder, the brass jumped
Into the snow.

        The tank was growing large.
The cannon flashed. Machinegun tracers curved
Toward it, and played sparkling on the steel.
Still it came on, glittering in return
From its machineguns. Then, a crashing flame
Struck it, leaving a trail of smoke in air.
The tank shuddered. It slewed broadside around.

Inside the plates, as on an anvil, hammers
Were laboring. It trembled with explosions,
And smoke poured out of it.

                              The slope was still,
Sprawling with hooded figures—and the rest
Gone back into the trees. Then there began
The sound of the wounded.

                              Dodd stood up
And looked around. In the next hole, a helmet
Moved cautiously.

                    "Lopez," he inquired,
"Are you all right?"

                         "Jesus!" the mailman said.

With a shaking hand, Dodd felt for cigarettes.
He breathed tobacco deep into his lungs.
On the twigs where he had left it balanced
His mug was hissing and—he held it—warm.

XII

Sometimes the snow came drifting down again.
And when it ceased, eddies and gusts of wind
Would lift it in long skirts that swept across
The dead. It packed into the stiffened folds
Of clothing. When night fell, a freezing wind
Encased the tree-trunks in bright sheathes of ice
And hung bright icicles on every branch,
And clamped the dead in rigid attitudes.

A shell came whistling down. The runner clenched
His fists. It crashed. Another shell came in.
The crashes jarred the ground. Then, from the rear,
A battery replied; shells fluttered back.

"Dodd!"

       He unzipped his bag, put on his helmet,
And stood.

         "Where are you?"

              It was the First Sergeant.

"Here," the runner answered.

             "Take this message
Back to Battalion. Are you listening?"

"Yes," he said.

        "To Colonel Jesserman.
The Captain says we need a fifty-seven
Or tank-destroyer. Tell him that it's urgent.
Now you repeat the message."

           Dodd did so.
He slung his rifle over his right shoulder
And climbed out of his hole.

           "Keep out of trouble,'
The sergeant said. "Don't stop for anything."
Dodd started to move off. The sergeant grasped
His arm: "Watch out! They may have got patrols
Between us and Battalion. Good luck!"

65

Dodd waved his hand, although it was too dark
For the other to see him. And set off
In what seemed to be the right direction.

Rome. December 2, 1957

Old Soldier

A dream of battle on a windy night
Has wakened him. The shadows move once more
With rumors of alarm. He sees the height
And helmet of his terror in the door.

The guns reverberate; a livid arc
From sky to sky lightens the windowpanes
And all his room. The clock ticks in the dark;
A cool wind stirs the curtains, and it rains.

He lies remembering: "That's how it was . . ."
And smiles, and drifts into a youthful sleep
Without a care. His life is all he has,
And that is given to the guards to keep.

The Bird

"Ich wünscht', ich wäre ein Vöglein,"
Sang Heinrich, "I would fly
Across the sea . . ." so sadly
It made his mother cry.

At night he played his zither,
By day worked in the mine.
His friend was Hans; together
The boys walked by the Rhine.

"Each day we're growing older,"
Hans said, "This is no life.
I wish I were a soldier!"
And snapped his pocket-knife.

War came, and Hans was taken,
But Heinrich did not fight.
"Ich wünscht', ich wäre ein Vöglein,"
Sang Heinrich every night.

"Dear Heinrich," said the letter,
"I hope this finds you fine.
The war could not be better,
It's women, song and wine."

A letter came for Heinrich,
The same that he'd sent East
To Hans, his own hand-writing
Returned, and marked *Deceased.*

*

"You'll never be a beauty,"
The doctor said, "You scamp!

We'll give you special duty—
A concentration camp."

And now the truck was nearing
The place. They passed a house;
A radio was blaring
The *Wiener Blut* of Strauss.

The banks were bright with flowers,
The birds sang in the wood;
There was a fence with towers
On which armed sentries stood.

They stopped. The men dismounted;
Heinrich got down—at last!
"That chimney," said the sergeant,
"That's where the Jews are gassed."

*

Each day he sorted clothing,
Skirt, trousers, boot and shoe,
Till he was filled with loathing
For every size of Jew.

"Come in! What is it, Private?"
"Please Sir, that vacancy . . .
I wonder, could I have it?"
"Your papers! Let me see . . .

"You're steady and you're sober . . .
But have you learned to kill?"
Said Heinrich, "No, *Herr Ober-
Leutnant,* but I will!"

"The Reich can use your spirit.
Report to Unit Four.
Here is an arm-band—wear it!
Dismissed! Don't slam the door."

*

"Ich wünscht', ich wäre ein Vöglein,"
Sang Heinrich, "I would fly . . ."
They knew that when they heard him
The next day they would die.

They stood in silence praying
At midnight when they heard
The zither softly playing,
The singing of the Bird.

He stared into the fire,
He sipped a glass of wine.
"Ich wünscht'," his voice rose higher,
"Ich wäre ein Vöglein . . ."

A dog howled in its kennel,
He thought of Hans and cried.
The stars looked down from heaven.
That day the children died.

*

"The Russian tanks are coming!"
The wind bore from the East
A cannonade, a drumming
Of small arms that increased.

Heinrich went to Headquarters.
He found the Colonel dead
With pictures of his daughters,
A pistol by his head.

He thought, his courage sinking,
"There's always the SS . . ."
He found the Major drinking
In a woman's party dress.

The prisoners were shaking
Their barracks. Heinrich heard
A sound of timber breaking,
A shout, "Where is the Bird?"

*

The Russian was completing
A seven-page report.
He wrote: "We still are beating
The woods . . ." then he stopped short.

A little bird was flitting
Outside, from tree to tree.
He turned where he was sitting
And watched it thoughtfully.

He pulled himself together,
And wrote: "We've left no stone
Unturned—but not a feather!
It seems the Bird has flown.

"Description? Half a dozen
Group snapshots, badly blurred;

And which is Emma's cousin
God knows, and which the Bird!

"He could be in the Western
Or in the Eastern Zone.
I'd welcome a suggestion
If anything is known."

*

"Ich wünscht', ich wäre ein Vöglein,"
Sings Heinrich, "I would fly
Across the sea," so sadly
It makes his children cry.

The Silent Generation

When Hitler was the Devil
He did as he had sworn
With such enthusiasm
That even, *donnerwetter,*
The Germans say, "Far better
Had he been never born!"

It was my generation
That put the Devil down
With great enthusiasm.
But now our occupation
Is gone. Our education
Is wasted on the town.

We lack enthusiasm.
Life seems a mystery;
It's like the play a lady
Told me about: "It's not . . .
It doesn't *have* a plot,"
She said, "It's history."

Against the Age

Under broad banners and barbarian
Words gather armies, as the liars wish.
And what's the aftermath? A murdered man,
A crying woman, and an empty dish.
Caesar rides cockhorse through triumphant Rome
And falls into a fit when he's at home.

Those banners fade behind that blew before,
The ships are rusting at the harbor wall,
And we will go to Normandy no more.
Clean up the streets and mop the city hall
And then go home. The war continues there
Against a vague and gathering despair.

Our minds are mutilated—*gueules cassées,*
They walk the night with hood and mask and stick,
The government won't let them out by day,
Their ugliness threatens the Republic.
Our minds are like those violated souls
That pass in faceless, threatening patrols.

Landscape and garden, village of the mind—
This is man's only state. Here he survives,
And only in a corner will he find
His happiness, if any. But our lives
Are lies of State, the slogans for today.
That wind is carrying the world away.

Carentan O Carentan

Trees in the old days used to stand
And shape a shady lane
Where lovers wandered hand in hand
Who came from Carentan.

This was the shining green canal
Where we came two by two
Walking at combat-interval.
Such trees we never knew.

The day was early June, the ground
Was soft and bright with dew.
Far away the guns did sound,
But here the sky was blue.

The sky was blue, but there a smoke
Hung still above the sea
Where the ships together spoke
To towns we could not see.

Could you have seen us through a glass
You would have said a walk
Of farmers out to turn the grass,
Each with his own hay-fork.

The watchers in their leopard suits
Waited till it was time,
And aimed between the belt and boot
And let the barrel climb.

I must lie down at once, there is
A hammer at my knee.
And call it death or cowardice,
Don't count again on me.

Everything's alright, Mother,
Everyone gets the same
At one time or another.
It's all in the game.

I never strolled, nor ever shall,
Down such a leafy lane.
I never drank in a canal,
Nor ever shall again.

There is a whistling in the leaves
And it is not the wind,
The twigs are falling from the knives
That cut men to the ground.

Tell me, Master-Sergeant,
The way to turn and shoot.
But the Sergeant's silent
That taught me how to do it.

O Captain, show us quickly
Our place upon the map.
But the Captain's sickly
And taking a long nap.

Lieutenant, what's my duty,
My place in the platoon?
He too's a sleeping beauty,
Charmed by that strange tune.

Carentan O Carentan
Before we met with you
We never yet had lost a man
Or known what death could do.

5. LOVE POEMS

Rough Winds Do Shake

Rough winds do shake
                  do shake
                                  the darling buds of May
The darling buds
                rose buds
                      the winds do shake
That are her breasts.
Those darling buds, dew-tipped, her sighing moods do
      shake.

She is sixteen
              sixteen
                    and her young lust
Is like a thorn
              hard thorn
                    among the pink
Of her soft nest.
Upon this thorn she turns, for love's incessant sake.

Her heart will break
                will break
                      unless she may
Let flow her blood
              red blood
                    to ease the ache
Where she is pressed.
Then she'll lie still, asleep, who now lies ill, awake.

Well, I have seen
                    have seen
                              one come to joust
Who has a horn
              sweet horn,
                          and spear to sink
Before he rests.
When such young buds are torn, the best true loves they
        make.

Summer Storm

In that so sudden summer storm they tried
Each bed, couch, closet, carpet, car-seat, table,
Both river banks, five fields, a mountain side,
Covering as much ground as they were able.

A lady, coming on them in the dark
In a white fixture, wrote to the newspapers
Complaining of the statues in the park.
By Cupid, but they cut some pretty capers!

The envious oxen in still rings would stand
Ruminating. Their sweet incessant plows
I think had changed the contours of the land
And made two modest conies move their house.

God rest them well, and firmly shut the door.
Now they are married Nature breathes once more.

The Traveler

Where are you going, Peter? sighed
    A cool and shady tree.
He took the question in his stride—
    I cannot stay, said he.

Where are you going, Peter? cried
    The fishes in the sea.
The moon, he said, that moves the tide,
    The moon is moving me.

My love is panting like a bride,
    Her laugh is low and free,
And I must hurry to her side
    Wherever she may be.

The Custom of the World

O, we loved long and happily, God knows!
The ocean danced, the green leaves tossed, the air
Was filled with petals, and pale Venus rose
When we began to kiss. Kisses brought care,
And closeness caused the taking off of clothes.
O, we loved long and happily, God knows!

"The watchdogs are asleep, the doormen doze. . . ."
We huddled in the corners of the stair,
And then we climbed it. What had we to lose?
What would we gain? The best way to compare
And quickest, was by taking off our clothes.
O, we loved long and happily, God knows!

Between us two a silent treason grows,
Our pleasures have been changed into despair.
Wild is the wind, from a cold country blows,
In which these tender blossoms disappear.
And did this come of taking off our clothes?
O, we loved long and happily, God knows!

Mistress, my song is drawing to a close.
Put on your rumpled skirt and comb your hair,
And when we meet again let us suppose
We never loved or ever naked were.
For though this nakedness was good, God knows,
The custom of the world is wearing clothes.

The Lover's Ghost

I fear the headless man
Whose military scars
Proclaim his merit.
And yet I fear a woman
More than the ghost of Mars,
A wounded spirit.

That look, all kindness lost,
Cold hands, as cold as stone,
A wanton gesture—
"What do you want, old ghost?
How long must I atone?"
So I addressed her.

"Did you not call?" she said,
"Goodbye, then! For I go
Where I am wanted."
Till dawn I tossed in bed
Wishing that I could know
Who else she haunted.

The Goodnight

He stood still by her bed
Watching his daughter breathe,
The dark and silver head,
The fingers curled beneath,
And thought: Though she may have
Intelligence and charm
And luck, they will not save
Her life from every harm.

The lives of children are
Dangerous to their parents
With fire, water, air,
And other accidents;
And some, for a child's sake,
Anticipating doom,
Empty the world to make
The world safe as a room.

Who could endure the pain
That was Laocoön's?
Twisting, he saw again
In the same coil his sons.
Plumed in his father's skill,
Young Icarus flew higher
Toward the sun, until
He fell in rings of fire.

A man who cannot stand
Children's perilous play,
With lifted voice and hand
Drives the children away.
Out of sight, out of reach,

The tumbling children pass;
He sits on an empty beach,
Holding an empty glass.

Who said that tenderness
Will turn the heart to stone?
May I endure her weakness
As I endure my own.
Better to say goodnight
To breathing flesh and blood
Each night as though the night
Were always only good.

Tom Pringle

The May moon rises bright and clear
Across the windowpane,
It brings the flowers every year
But not my loves again.
I too have heard the melody
That lovers like to hear;
I slept, I dreamed in Arcady,
I woke, and I was there.

The joys we had, the joys we miss,
Take all our joy away,
And many who were glad to kiss
Are now content to pray.
Their heaven is a hospital,
Their piety a crutch;
They don't appeal to me at all,
I like the world too much.

I will not jar the stars with praise
In silence as they sing;
To tell eternity to days
Might swerve an angel's wing.
But I will watch the comets' flight
And not a cloud between
From perfect day to perfect night
And wonder what they mean.

THE WESLEYAN POETRY PROGRAM

Distinguished contemporary poetry in cloth and paperback editions

ALAN ANSEN: *Disorderly Houses* (1961)

JOHN ASHBERY: *The Tennis Court Oath* (1962)

ROBERT BAGG: *Madonna of the Cello* (1961)

ROBERT BLY: *Silence in the Snowy Fields* (1962)

TURNER CASSITY: *Watchboy, What of the Night?* (1966)

TRAM COMBS: *saint thomas. poems.* (1965)

DONALD DAVIE: *Events and Wisdoms* (1965): *New and Selected Poems* (1961)

JAMES DICKEY: *Buckdancer's Choice* (1965) [National Book Award in Poetry, 1966]; *Drowning With Others* (1962); *Helmets* (1964)

DAVID FERRY: *On the Way to the Island* (1960)

ROBERT FRANCIS: *The Orb Weaver* (1960)

JOHN HAINES: *Winter News* (1966)

RICHARD HOWARD: *The Damages* (1967); *Quantities* (1962)

BARBARA HOWES: *Light and Dark* (1959)

DAVID IGNATOW: *Figures of the Human* (1964); *Say Pardon* (1961)

DONALD JUSTICE: *Night Light* (1967); *The Summer Anniversaries* (1960) [A Lamont Poetry Selection]

CHESTER KALLMAN: *Absent and Present* (1963)

LOU LIPSITZ: *Cold Water* (1967)

JOSEPHINE MILES: *Kinds of Affection* (1967)

VASSAR MILLER: *My Bones Being Wiser* (1963); *Wage War on Silence* (1960)

W. R. MOSES: *Identities* (1965)

DONALD PETERSEN: *The Spectral Boy* (1964)

HYAM PLUTZIK: *Apples from Shinar* (1959)

VERN RUTSALA: *The Window* (1964)

HARVEY SHAPIRO: *Battle Report* (1966)

JON SILKIN: *Poems New and Selected* (1966)

LOUIS SIMPSON: *At the End of the Open Road* (1963) [Pulitzer Prize in Poetry, 1964]; *A Dream of Governors* (1959)

JAMES WRIGHT: *The Branch Will Not Break* (1963); *Saint Judas* (1959)